The

Road

To

Self-Publishing

(Navigating the self-publishing journey)

Mathew Thomas

Table of Contents

PREFACE

AS A WRITER, YOU HAVE a story, a message to share, or a world to create. But the path to becoming a published author can be overwhelming and confusing. From drafting your manuscript to designing your cover and formatting your book, self-publishing can seem daunting, especially for first-time authors.

This book, "Road to Self-Publishing: Navigating the self-publishing journey," is designed to be your roadmap to navigating the self-publishing process. In these pages, you'll find guidance, insights, and practical advice to help you take control of your publishing journey and achieve your goals as an independent author.

This book is a simple but comprehensive guide to self-publishing, drawing on my experience as an indie author. As you're just starting your writing journey, you'll find valuable insights and strategies on these pages to help you succeed.

From generating book ideas to writing the book and submitting it to publishing, this book covers everything you need to know to create a successful and sustainable writing career. Actionable advice, tips, and resources to help you navigate the self-publishing process with confidence and ease are provided in each chapter.

So, whether you're writing a memoir, a novel, or a self-help book or publishing your work in ebook, or paperback format, this book is here to help you drive your way to become a successful indie author. The road to self-publishing can be challenging, but with the right tools and mindset, you can achieve your dreams of sharing your story with the world. The book aims to simplify the process and remove confusion and complexity, ultimately building confidence for first-time writers. It draws on familiar concepts and strategies that you can use to achieve writing objectives.

When I first started writing, I was overwhelmed and intimidated by the writing process. Breaking down complex concepts and simplifying them can help make the process more approachable and achievable. Questions such as, "Do I need special writing tools?" "Should I risk a considerable investment, and is it worth the expense, or should I skimp on high costs?" "Do I wait to see the results and gradually fine-tune the actions, or do I jump right in with all I have and hope it will pay off?" all bothered me. Therefore, I felt the burden of breaking the process down for aspiring writers and hope their journey would be less daunting and more pleasant.

I aim to help aspiring writers build confidence and feel empowered to pursue their writing goals. Writing is a rewarding and fulfilling journey, but it can be challenging to navigate, especially for beginners. With this book, I hope to make the process more accessible and enjoyable for everyone who dreams of writing a book. Remember, the most important thing is to start. Don't let fear or self-doubt hold you back. With the right mindset and tools, you can overcome any obstacle and achieve your writing objectives.

Buckle up, stomp the peddle and let's hit the road together on a journey of excellent writing experience!

CHAPTER 1: INTRODUCTION

WELCOME TO THE WORLD of independent writing! It's a brave new world, full of opportunities and possibilities, and you're about to embark on an exciting journey. Whether you've always dreamed of writing a book or have just recently discovered your passion for writing, this guide is designed to help you take your first steps toward becoming an indie author.

Writing your first book is an exciting journey that will take you on a roller coaster ride of emotions. From the exhilaration of coming up with a great idea, to the frustration of writer's block, to the joy of finally holding your finished product in your hands, it's a journey that will test your patience, creativity, and perseverance.

This guide will look at practical tips and techniques to help you start your writing journey. We'll also discuss some common challenges that indie writers face and provide advice on overcoming them. Our goal is to help you build your confidence as a writer and to help you realise your dream of writing your first book. Whether you're an experienced writer looking to branch out into self-publishing or a first-time writer with a great idea, the tips and strategies in this book will help you start writing and stay motivated until you finish.

Why Write?

Before we dive into the nuts and bolts of writing, let's take a step back and consider why you want to write in the first place. There are many reasons why people choose to write, and each person's motivation is unique. Some people write to express themselves, explore creativity, or share ideas. Others write to inspire, entertain, or educate their readers. Whatever your reasons for writing, it's important to remember them as you embark on your writing journey.

Getting Started

One of the biggest challenges that first-time indie writers face is getting started. It's easy to feel overwhelmed by the prospect of writing a book and to put it off indefinitely. However, the key to success as a writer is to start writing. You don't need a fully formed idea or a detailed outline. All you need is a blank page and a willingness to express your thoughts.

Writing can be daunting, especially if you're unsure where to start. But do not worry! You do not need fancy tools or expensive software to write your first book. You only need a computer, a word processor, and a desire to tell your story. If you are passionate about fulfilling your wishes without being overwhelmed by the process, this book is for you. We will focus on readily available tools and consider only the minimum basic requirements while avoiding using fancy styles you can use in future books once you are established.

To get started, find a quiet place where you can focus and set aside some dedicated time to write each day. Depending on your schedule and availability, this can be as little as fifteen minutes or as much as several hours.

In this book, we'll cover the basics of writing, including how to write, revise and edit your work. We'll also discuss the ins and outs of self-publishing, including how to format your book, design a cover, and some basics of marketing your book once it's published. This book does not suggest what you should write or the linguistic skills needed to be adopted. However, understanding the nitty-gritty of the writing environment can help you so that the process involved doesn't bog down your passion for telling the story.

But before we dive into the specifics of writing and self-publishing, let's talk about the most important thing you need to become a successful indie author: confidence.

Building Confidence as an Indie Writer

A lack of confidence is one of the first-time indie authors' biggest hurdles. Writing a book can be intimidating, especially when surrounded by many talented writers and successful authors who can intimidate you. But the truth is, every writer has to start somewhere. Moreover, the abundance of tools available for writing, editing, proofreading, cover design, self-publishing, and marketing can be so confusing that you might question whether the cost and effort are worth it. Many books on the subject only add to the burden of already-existing self-doubt. This book aims to take the first step and navigate the writing process without wondering which tools to use or how much to spend to become a writer.

Throughout this book, all references to self-publishing refer to KDP Amazon Publishing. You may apply the principles for other platforms, but we will restrict our discussion to Amazon for this book.

CHAPTER 2: WHAT BOOK?

WRITING A BOOK CAN be overwhelming, but breaking it down into smaller, more manageable steps can make it much more achievable. In this chapter, we'll explore three crucial elements of book content: identifying the subject of your book, brainstorming ideas and developing your concept, and outlining your book.

Identifying the subject of your book is the first step in the writing process. This involves determining what you want your book to be about. Choosing a topic you're passionate about and have expertise in is essential. Writing a book is a significant investment of time and energy, so you want to ensure that the subject you choose is something you're excited to write about and will keep you engaged throughout the writing process. You must think of a catchy and relevant title for the content body.

Make a list of three or four titles and search for any books on Amazon with these titles. If any of those titles exist, you don't want to infringe on them unless they are successful, and you may benefit from spill-over. But the reverse can be disastrous. You can, of course, change your title later or just before publishing. But to begin with, a title can be a morale booster.

Once you have identified the subject of your book, the next step is to brainstorm ideas and develop your concept. Brainstorming is generating ideas without worrying about whether they're good or bad. It's a way to get your creative juices flowing and develop various ideas to explore further. These ideas can be fleeting and therefore need to be captured as soon as they pop into your head. Use the Office tool, OneNote, to capture these thoughts. OneNote is available across all devices and is cloud-based, allowing perfect syncing. So when an idea or thought pops up, whether on a bus or a flight, pull out your mobile phone and record that in OneNote. Please don't wait for your flight to land and reach home to open your laptop and record it. That thought travels faster than the plane and would have left you long before realising it. If you are familiar with other note-taking tools like EverNote, you may use them instead of OneNote. Once you've generated a list of ideas, you can begin to refine them and develop a concept for your book.

Developing a concept for your book involves clarifying your ideas and figuring out how they fit together. It's helpful to think about your book in terms of its central message or theme. What do you want your readers to take away from your book? What is the big idea that ties everything together? Your concept will help guide you as you begin to develop your outline.

Outlining your book is the third step in developing your book's content. An outline is a roadmap for your book. It's a way to organise your ideas and ensure that your book flows logically from beginning to end. Your outline should include an introduction, several chapters that explore different aspects of your subject, and a conclusion that ties everything together.

As you develop your outline, thinking about your target audience is helpful. Who are you writing this book for? What are their needs and interests? Keeping your audience in mind will help you create a book that is engaging and relevant to your readers.

In addition to organising your ideas, your outline can help you identify any gaps in your content. Are there areas that need more research or development? Are there topics that you need to explore further? Your outline will help you identify these gaps to fill them in as you write your book.

In conclusion, by identifying the subject of your book, brainstorming ideas and developing your concept, and outlining your book, you'll be well on your way to creating a book that's engaging, relevant, and informative. Remember to stay focused on your audience, and don't be afraid to refine and revise your ideas as you go along. Writing a book is a challenging but rewarding process, and by breaking it down into smaller steps, you can make it much more achievable.

CHAPTER 3: WRITING YOUR BOOK

THE WRITING ENVIRONMENT

Writing is a beautiful and fulfilling craft that has captured the imagination of people for centuries. Whether it is writing a novel, a screenplay, a blog post, or an academic paper, the written word has the power to move, inspire, educate, and entertain. However, writing is not easy, especially for first-time writers who may feel overwhelmed and lost in the vast and complex writing world. That is why every writer must know about the writing environment, the tools and options available, and the best practices to follow.

The writing environment is the space and context in which writers create their work. It includes the physical and mental space, the tools and resources, and the social and cultural context that shapes the writer's process and product. To create an optimal writing environment, first-time writers must consider several factors, such as the location, the time, and the equipment.

The location of the writing space can have a significant impact on the quality and quantity of writing. Ideally, the writing space should be quiet, comfortable, and free of distractions. A quiet room can help writers focus and concentrate, while a comfortable space can help them feel relaxed and inspired.

Furthermore, a distraction-free space can help writers stay on track and avoid procrastination.

The time of day is also essential when creating a writing environment. Some writers prefer to write early in the morning when their mind is fresh and clear, while others prefer to write late at night when the world is quiet and still. Whatever the time of day, it is essential to set aside a specific time for writing and stick to it consistently.

The equipment and tools writers use can also significantly impact their writing process and product. In the digital age, writers can use numerous software and apps to enhance their writing experiences, such as word processors, note-taking apps, research tools, and productivity apps. These tools can help writers organise their ideas, improve their writing skills, and increase productivity.

However, choosing the right tools and options that suit the writer's needs and preferences is important. For example, some writers may prefer to use a traditional pen and paper to brainstorm and draft their ideas, while others may choose to use a digital tool that can help them save time and effort. Moreover, writers need to be familiar with the basic functions of their devices and learn how to use them effectively.

Aside from the physical and technical aspects of the writing environment, writers also need to be aware of the social and cultural context in which they write. Writing is not an isolated activity but rather a social and cultural practice that is influenced by various factors such as language, genre, audience, and purpose. Therefore, writers must consider their audience's social and cultural norms and expectations and adjust their writing accordingly.

For example, if a writer is writing a scientific paper, they need to use formal language and follow the conventions of the scientific community. On the other hand, if a writer writes a blog post, they can use a more informal and conversational tone that appeals to a broader audience. Furthermore, writers must know their audience's cultural differences and sensitivities and avoid offensive or inappropriate content.

Many YouTubers and books will suggest specific tools to help you put your ideas into writing. Many word processors on the market are fine-tuned for writers, such as Reedsy Book Editor, Draft, Mellel, Ulysses, and Scrivener, to name a few. But this is just the beginning of the list. Organisers, to-do apps, time-management tools, and soundtracks to soothe your mind while you work on writing are also available.

In this book, we will keep things simple and use tools that are familiar and used daily. The purpose of this book is not to downgrade the advanced tools that are great for writers who spend a lot of time writing. These tools can be very productive and help you focus on your content. However, these tools can be daunting for first-time writers, resulting in a steep learning curve and high cost.

By the end of this book, you will have gained the knowledge and confidence necessary to start your writing journey. You will have a solid understanding of the writing process and the tools available. Whether you use a simple word processor or an advanced writing tool, you will have the skills to produce high-quality writing. So, let's get started on this exciting adventure of self-discovery and creativity!

This book explores ordinary and everyday avenues to help you get started on your writing journey without spending too much money or time. The focus will be on using tools that we are familiar with and honing them to meet our writing needs. We will specifically consider MS Word, the most popular and widely-used processor, and study its formatting approach that will turn your book into an eBook or paperback for self-publishing. The idea is to invest minimally, spend less time learning the technical details, and get straight into your passion with confidence.

So you are all ready to start with your very first book.

Write your book with Word; it's your story's best sword!

This section will familiarise you with the process involved in producing an eBook. Once we know the method, we will apply the procedure for the paperback version of your book. So, all steps suggested in the following few paragraphs are related to eBooks only. We will list the additional process to be applied for paperback towards the end of this section.

We are all familiar with Microsoft Word, a popular word processor. If you already use Word, it's the perfect tool to start with as it doesn't require any additional cost and has a shorter learning curve, allowing you to focus on your writing goals. This section will cover the formatting needed for your work's eBook and paperback editions. It's important to remember to save your work regularly and create backups on external media, preferably using a cloud-based backup system, as you write. A computer failure should not be a cause of regret for all the time and effort put in.

To begin, let's open Word to a blank document. This is your slate where your ideas and thoughts will turn into impactful words. Your ideas, a bundle of bits and pieces, will soon get organised and folded into a polished finished product. You are now staring at that blank board, waiting to transform your creativity into a popular format for others to read. But before you hit the keyboard with the very first character of your book, you need to set up Word.

You will divide your book into all or some of the following sections –

Title Page

Copyright page

Acknowledgements

Table of Contents

Chapters

Footnotes

Appendix

Notes

The main body of text will be the most dominant portion of your document and will follow a standard style. The Chapter numbers and headings will require a different style. So to begin, we will set up the Styles you will use in your document.

<u>Setting Styles</u>

First, we will set the font type, size, justification, paragraph indentation, and spacing for each required style in our document.

Figure 1

Under Home Menu – Styles section, right-click the Normal button and select Modify.

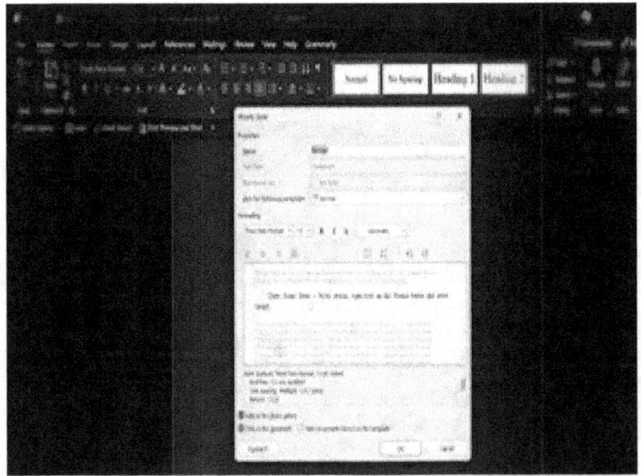

Figure 2

The Modify Style box will appear as in Figure 2. You can select the font, size, and justification type under the formatting options. You can also set additional options according to your writing style under the Format drop-down box at the bottom. Once you have made your changes, click <OK> to commit them.

Using the Normal style throughout the document's body of the text is best. Whenever you type regular text, make sure that the Normal style button is selected. This will ensure that the font, paragraph settings, and justification type are all automatically applied.

Similarly, modify settings for Heading 1, Heading 2, and, if required Heading 3 styles. Chapter numbers, Chapter headings, and sub-headings can use Heading styles. Set the font type and size and other parameters under each Heading style. Applying the Heading style to Chapters automatically allows you to create a Table of Contents.

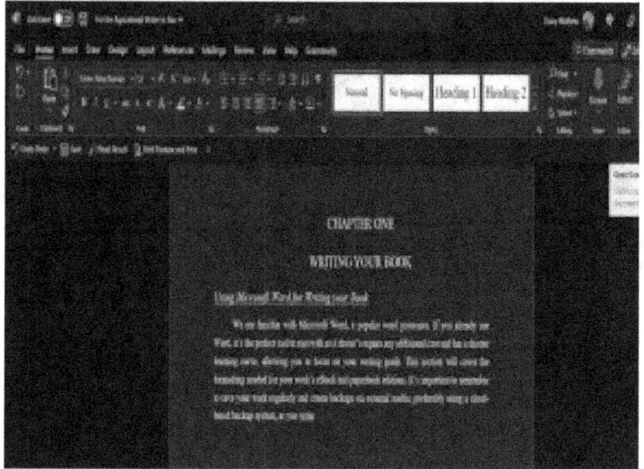

Figure 3

In Figure 3, CHAPTER ONE uses the Heading 1 style. The heading for this chapter – WRITING YOUR BOOK – uses Heading 2 style, and the sub-heading – *Using Microsoft Word for Writing your Book* – uses Heading 3 style. We will try to understand the use of multiple headings' significance when dealing with the Table of Contents.

Once you have set your styles, you can start writing the book.

The formatting of your book in Word will depend on whether you are writing for an eBook or a paperback publication. First, create the eBook edition of your book and name the document as <Title of the Book – eBook Edition>. Once you have completed your writing, save the document as another copy <Title of the Book – Paperback Edition>. You should have two versions of your book on your computer - eBook and paperback. Both will have identical content, so making a paperback copy should only be done once you have completed the book writing. If you make changes to the content in any document, make those changes in the other copy too. You can then proceed to format each according to the requirements for self-publishing. As we continue in this chapter, we will understand the formatting for each edition of the book.

The font type and size are left to the choice of the writer. However, using fonts under the serif fonts category, which includes Times New Roman, Garamond, Courier New etc., is best. These fonts have small features at the ends of strokes compared to sans-serif, which lack those strokes – F (serif); F (sans-serif). For this book, I have used Times New Roman with a font size of 12. I suggest staying with a standard serif font when modifying the style settings.

<u>Page Breaks</u>

Page breaks are essential for starting text on a new page in Word. You can insert a page break by clicking the "Insert" menu and selecting "Page break." Avoid using the Enter key multiple times to move to the next page; instead, insert a page break at the end of the previous page. This way, your text will start on a new page. However, don't insert a page break after every page if your text is continuous. Only use page breaks when you want the subsequent text to start on a new page.

When you convert your Word document to Kindle eBook format, keep in mind that the total number of lines per page may not match the Word page. So, the text that appears on one page in Word may spill over to the next page on Kindle. If you insert a page break at the end of every page, the text on the next page may appear continuous in Word. But when you convert it to Kindle format, the text will move to the next page, resulting in a broken appearance. Therefore, only insert page breaks where you want the text to start on a new page in Kindle. You can use page breaks for the beginnings of new chapters or sections, separating the Title page and copyright page, and the start of the Table of Contents.

Identifying Page Breaks

To identify the location of page breaks, click on the paragraph symbol - ¶. The page break marks will appear in their designated places.

Chapters, Headings, and sub-headings

Before beginning a new chapter and at the end of the previous chapter, insert a page break. Your chapters may contain the chapter number and chapter heading.

CHAPTER ONE

HEADING FOR THE CHAPTER

If you intend to display the chapter number and heading on two separate lines in your Table of Contents page, use the Heading 1 style for the chapter number and the Heading 2 style for the chapter heading. You Can display the Table of Contents on multiple levels. Figures 4, 5, and 6 are examples of multi-level displays of the Table of Contents.

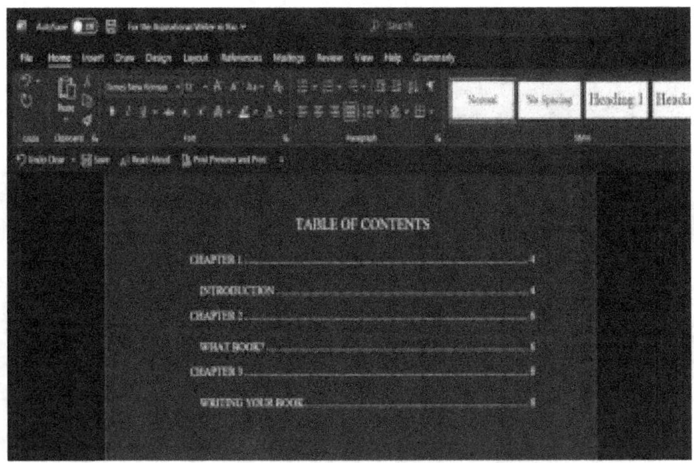

Figure 4 (Two levels)

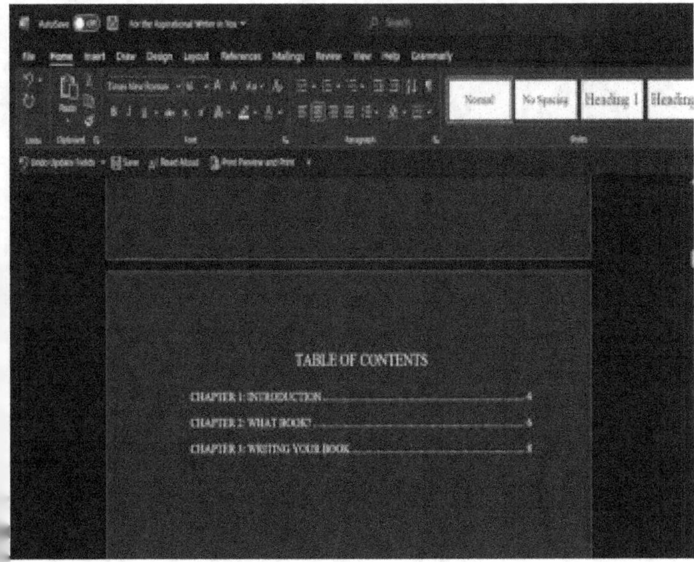

Figure 5 (Single level)

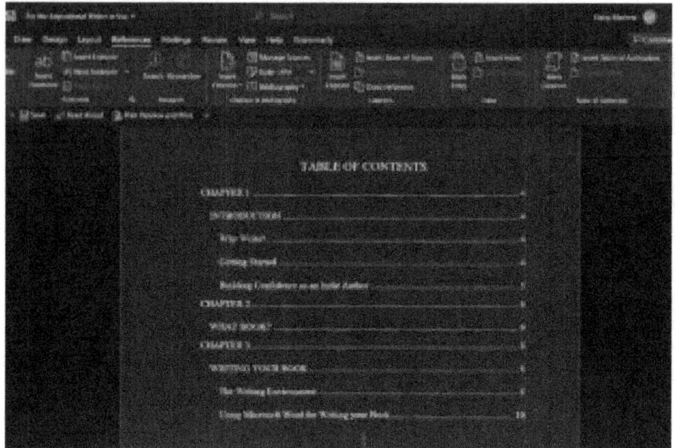

Figure 6 (Three levels)

The three-level Table of Contents (Figure 6) uses three Heading styles. The Chapter number uses Heading 1, the Chapter heading, Heading 2, and the sub-heading, Heading 3. In the same way in Figure 5, there is only one level, and both the chapter number and chapter heading use the Heading 1 style. You must update the Table of Contents field whenever you add a new chapter or modify the chapter numbers and heading.

How to create a Table of Contents

Open a blank page at the top following the copyright and acknowledgements pages. Type the title for the page. The title could be – Table of Contents, Contents, Index, etc. Press Enter key.

Click <References> <Table of Contents drop down> <Custom Table of Contents ...>

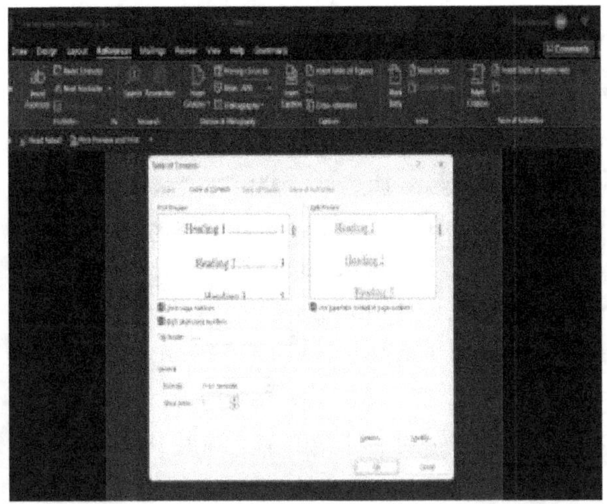

Figure 7

For eBooks, untick "Show Page numbers" and tick "Use hyperlinks instead of page numbers.". For paperback, tick "Show Page numbers" and untick "Use hyperlinks instead of page numbers.". Select the number of levels appearing by default depending on the number of Heading styles used in your document. Click <Modify> <Modify> and set the font, size, justification, and other values per your choice.

Click <OK> to insert the Table of Contents.

Remember to update the Table after chapter numbers and heading changes and before final publishing. To update, highlight the Table of Contents, right-click, and click <Update field>.

Headers and Footers

The eBook version does not require any Headers or Footers.

For the paperback version, use footers to display Page numbers and headers to display the book title. Click on <Insert> <Header> <Edit Header>. In the Header box, tick on the "Different First page" if you don't want to display any header on the first page, typically the Title page or a completely different header for the first page. Tick "Different Odd and Even pages" to display different headers for the odd and even pages. For example, display the book title on the even pages and the author's name on the odd pages or leave the odd page header blank.

Page Layout and Footnotes

Ensure that chapters begin on an odd page number for the paperback version. This may require you to skip a blank page between two chapters, especially when one chapter ends on an odd page. Insert page breaks at the end of the chapter and before the following chapter. To skip and create a blank page, insert one more page break.

For the eBook version, use Insert Endnote, and for the paperback version, use Insert Footnote. When you publish your book as an eBook, the system converts all footnotes to endnotes. Endnotes appear at the end of the book, whereas footnotes appear at the foot of the respective pages.

For paperback, page layout becomes especially important. KDP Amazon offers a wide range of book sizes, also known as trim sizes, to choose from. Trim size is the printed book's width and height. The trim size you choose determines the book's total page numbers and will affect the overall cover design. The most common trim size for paperbacks in the US is 6 x 9 inches. Other sizes include in inches – 5 x 8, 5.25 x 8, 5.5 x 8.5, 7 x 10 and others. We will consider 5 x 8 inches for this book as our trim size.

Once you decide on the trim size, you must format your Word document accordingly. Open the paperback version of your Word document if you have created one. If not, "save as" the document with the name <Title of book – paperback edition>.

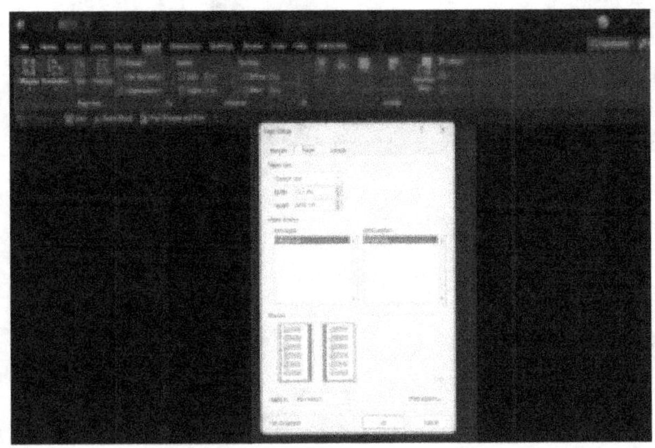

Figure 8

Click <Layout> <Margins> <Custom Margins ...> <Paper Tab>. Enter the width and height of the trim size selected in inches or cm depending on your Word document system. For a 5 x 8 inches, enter width as 5 (12.7 cms) and height as 8 (20.32 cms). In the preview box below, select The Whole Document in Apply to drop down and click <OK>. See Figure 8.

Now click on the Margins Tab and enter values for the margin and gutter, as seen in Figure 9 below –

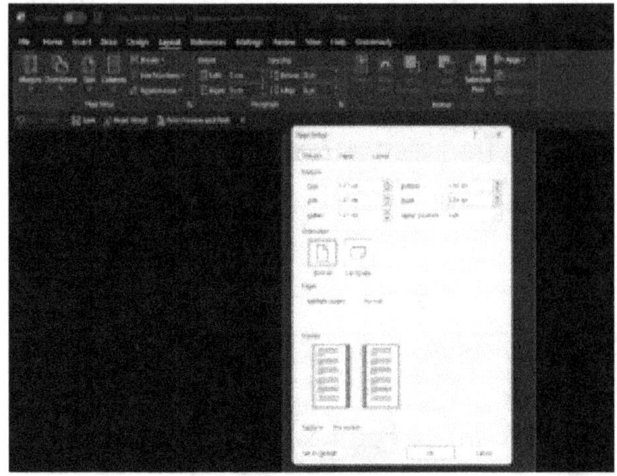

Figure 9

Please enter a margin of at least 0.5 inches (1.27 cm) for the top, bottom, left, and right, and use 0.5 inches (1.27 cm) for the gutter. The gutter is the area between the two pages as we open a book.

<u>Final Checklist</u>

Finally, before you commit the book to self-publishing, the final checklist should include the following –

For eBook version -

1. Click on the paragraph symbol ¶ to check appropriate page breaks are inserted.
2. Update the Table of Contents.

For the paperback version –

1. Click on the paragraph symbol ¶ to check appropriate page breaks are inserted.
2. Ensure all chapters begin on the odd page numbers for the paperback version.
3. Update the Table of Contents.
4. Check page number appears as Footer in its proper location.
5. Ensure Headers appear as required.
6. Confirm that you have correctly set the page layout, paper size, and margins according to your requirements.

34

CHAPTER 4: REVISING YOUR WRITING

CONGRATULATIONS! YOU have made it through the daunting task of writing your book. But the journey is not over yet. The next step is revising your work to ensure it is polished and ready for publication. This chapter will explore changing your draft through the proofreading and editing stages.

Proofreading is the first step in revising your work. It is the process of carefully reviewing your manuscript to identify and correct grammar, spelling, punctuation, and formatting errors. Proofreading is crucial in ensuring your work is error-free and easy to read.

While proofreading by hand is an effective way to catch errors, it can be time-consuming and tedious. Fortunately, Microsoft Word has a built-in editor to help you see mistakes quickly and efficiently.

To use the built-in editor, click the "Review" tab in Word and select "Spelling & Grammar." Word will automatically scan your document for errors and highlight them in different colours, depending on the type of error. For example, Word will underline misspelled words in red and grammatical mistakes in green.

To review the errors Word identifies, right-click on the highlighted word or phrase. A menu will appear, offering suggestions for corrections. You can accept the suggestion, ignore the error, or make your correction.

In addition to the built-in editor, Word also provides various other tools to help you proofread. For example, the "Thesaurus" tool can help you find alternative words for repetitive phrases. Click the "Review" and select the "Editor" button for more advanced features. An editor window will appear to the right, as in Figure 10 below –

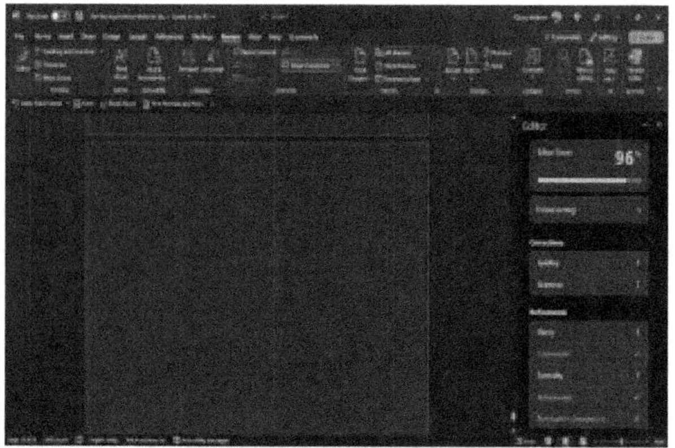

Figure 10

The Editor provides various functionalities that depend on the writing style. It offers three writing types to choose from – Formal, Professional, and Casual. Select the type that suits your writing and reader preferences the most. The Editor provides corrections for spelling and grammar, refinements for clarity, conciseness, formality, punctuation conventions, and more. Each function on the right-side box displays the number of errors that require revision. Click on each option to evaluate the response provided, which you can accept or ignore.

While the built-in editor can be helpful, it is important to note that it is not foolproof. It may miss errors or make suggestions inappropriate for your writing style or tone. That is why it is important to use the built-in editor as a tool in combination with other proofreading methods. In addition to reading your work aloud and having someone else review it, you can also use some advanced tools. We will look at one such tool later in the chapter.

Revising your work through proofreading and editing is essential in creating a polished and engaging manuscript. Using a combination of methods, such as proofreading by hand and using the built-in editor of Word or other tools, you can catch errors and refine your writing to make it clear, concise, and engaging for your readers. Take your time, be thorough, and your hard work will pay off.

The next step in revising your work is editing. Editing is refining your manuscript to ensure it is clear, concise, and engaging. This step involves reworking sentences, paragraphs, and chapters to make them more readable and compelling.

Begin by reading your manuscript aloud. This will help you identify awkward sentences or sections that do not flow well. As you read, take notes on areas that need improvement. Look for repetitive phrases, unclear ideas, and weak transitions that need strengthening. The built-in editor or more advanced tools can be valuable in identifying errors and corrections. In Figure 10, the refinements section can open areas where clarity, conciseness, and formality improvement can be hugely beneficial.

Once you have identified areas that need improvement, start reworking your manuscript. Ensure that your ideas are clearly expressed by improving sentence structure and flow. Consider adding descriptive language and examples to make your work more engaging.

As you edit, keep your audience in mind. Is your work accessible to readers who may not be familiar with your subject matter? Is your tone appropriate for your audience? Write your work while keeping your readers in mind.

After proofreading and editing, it is time to take a final look at your manuscript before self-publishing. Take a break from your work for a few days or even a week. When you return to it, you have fresh eyes to catch any last-minute errors.

Polish your prose with Grammarly: Your writing's new best friend!

Proofreading and editing by oneself or using the built-in editor of Microsoft Word have their limitations. The best option would be to outsource the task to online freelancers who can perform the work for a fee. Websites like Fiverr.com host several editors who can complete the job within a stipulated timeframe. However, they can also be costly as they charge by the word. The next best option and a writer's best friend is the powerful Grammarly software available at grammarly.com.

Don't let your book fall short; let Grammarly provide the support! Skip the pricey freelancers and editing strife, perfect your writing quickly, and enjoy a better life! That is Grammarly for you.

You can download Grammarly for free with limited functionalities or subscribe to the premium version. If language assistance is essential to your work, I strongly recommend subscribing to the paid version, as it is worth the investment.

After downloading and installing Grammarly, you must create a new account on the Grammarly site. You can then configure Grammarly for your specific writing needs. Log in to the site, click 'Account', then select 'Customize' and choose your language. Select your primary language, which I assume is English, and the English type - American, British, Canadian, Australian, or Indian.

After clicking on 'Writing Preferences,' a list of over forty preferences will appear under multiple categories such as Clarity, Correctness, Consistency, Punctuation, Formality, and more, all set to 'On' by default. I suggest you leave them all On; you can revisit them later and switch off specific preferences if needed.

Once you open your document in Word, Grammarly will appear as a menu option, and a box will pop up to the right where errors and suggested corrections are displayed as you type into Word. You may choose to accept the modifications or ignore the error. First, click the 'Grammarly' menu and select 'Adjust Goals'. You can tailor the application to make suggestions based on your goals and readers. Choose the kind of audience (readers), the formality level, and the domain you are writing in (See Figure 11). You may need to adjust your goals for each book you write based on the type of readership and the domain in which you are writing.

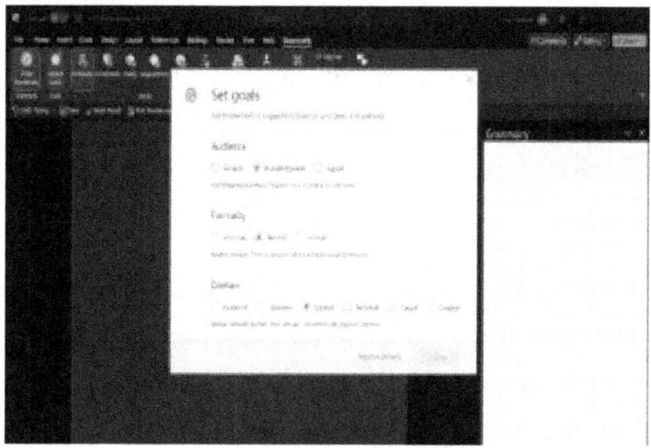

Figure 11

You are ready to use Grammarly's powerful features to transform your ordinary writing into more polished and professional work. Grammarly works in two ways: it displays errors and correct options, and you can click the right choice to replace the mistake in your text.

However, if your sentences are too wordy or monotonous or written in passive voice, Grammarly may point out these deviations without correcting them. It is up to the writer to make the necessary changes. Your completed work should ideally not have any issues appearing in the Grammarly box.

Another compelling feature is checking for plagiarism. Grammarly will check for plagiarism in your text by comparing it with billions of web pages and documents, highlighting passages that require citations, and giving you the resources you need to credit your sources appropriately. This is a very useful feature as it saves you from copyright infringement in your work.

Seeking help from Artificial Intelligence

Artificial Intelligence (AI) is revolutionizing the way we live, work, and interact with each other. With its ability to learn from data, automate tasks, and make predictions, AI has become a game-changer in various fields, from healthcare to finance, transportation to manufacturing, and beyond. In education, AI has made learning more accessible and personalized. Adaptive learning platforms powered by AI algorithms can tailor teaching to the needs of individual students, providing them with personalized feedback, recommendations, and resources. With AI taking over mundane activities, we should explore the opportunities to use AI to our advantage and work with it to develop new opportunities in writing.

You may wonder what role AI can play in a writer's life. It can be of great assistance to Indie writers in several ways. One of the most powerful AI tools available to one and all is the recent launch of ChatGPT.

Idea Generation: ChatGPT can assist in generating new and creative ideas for storylines, characters, and plot twists. By inputting a prompt or a few keywords related to the story, ChatGPT can provide a range of potential ideas to explore.

Writing Assistance: ChatGPT can help with writing assistance by suggesting synonyms, correcting grammar and punctuation, and providing alternate sentence structures. By giving a few sentences or paragraphs, ChatGPT can provide feedback and suggestions to help improve the quality of the writing.

Research Assistance: ChatGPT can also help with research assistance by providing links to relevant sources, fact-checking information, and providing additional context to support the writer's work.

Marketing Assistance: ChatGPT can assist with marketing by providing insights and tips on marketing a book, identifying target audiences, and generating promotional content.

AI, such as ChatGPT, can be a valuable tool for indie writers seeking to enhance their writing and effectively market their work. ChatGPT can act as your artificial freelance editor, proofreading and editing your work in a manner that exceeds your expectations. When used with Grammarly, these tools can elevate your writing creativity to new heights. ChatGPT can effortlessly correct errors identified by Grammarly, eliminating the need for manual corrections. For instance, if Grammarly highlights a sentence as being in the passive voice and suggests converting it to active voice, you can copy and paste the sentence into ChatGPT's query box and request it to correct the sentence to active voice. You can then copy it back into your text. Figure 12 below is an example of asking ChatGPT to convert a sentence from passive to active voice.

To access ChatGPT, please type the URL https://chat.openai.com in your browser. You must register before proceeding if this is your first time using ChatGPT. Once registered, you can type your request into the query box to receive a response. If you need to edit a paragraph in your document, copy and paste the paragraph into the query box and type "Proofread and Edit". Similarly, if you need to change a sentence from passive to active voice, copy and paste the sentence into the query box and type "Convert to active voice".

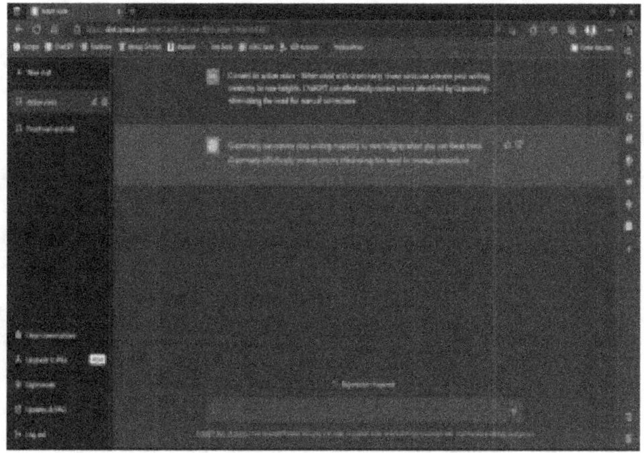

Figure 12

Each time you initiate a new chat, ChatGPT will assign a name to the chat, which will appear on the left panel (Figure 12). However, you can rename it according to your preference. You can use this feature to organize your tasks and easily switch between different chats. For example, you can have a chat named "Proofread and Edit" to check for errors and a chat called "Active Voice" to convert sentences to active voice. By selecting the appropriate chat and pasting your text into the query box, ChatGPT will automatically detect any errors and suggest corrections or convert the sentence to the active voice without requiring you to remind it each time. You can save time and increase productivity when working on language-related tasks.

Go ahead and use the power of ChatGPT; it is entirely free and has the potential to build your confidence in fulfilling your passion for writing.

Friendly Review

Finally, your book is ready, edited by technology through Grammarly and ChatGPT. We need some human touch to your work. Prepare your book's pdf files and send them to friends and family for their review, feedback, and suggestions.

As a writer, seeking feedback on your manuscript before publishing it is common. One way to do this is by sending the finished book to friends and family for review. Here are some things to keep in mind when doing so:

Choose your reviewers carefully: Not everyone can give feedback on your work. Choosing people who are familiar with your writing style and genre or know you well and who will provide constructive criticism rather than just praise is essential. Additionally, make sure your reviewers are willing to commit the time and effort needed to provide thorough feedback.

Give clear instructions: Provide your reviewers with clear guidelines on what you are looking for regarding feedback. Do you want them to focus on character development, pacing, or overall story arc? Do you want them to proofread or evaluate your content? Make sure they understand what you are looking for so they can provide the most helpful feedback possible.

Be open to criticism: It can be difficult to hear negative feedback about your work, but it is important to remember that criticism can help you improve as a writer. Be open to feedback, and don't take it personally. Instead, use it to identify areas where you can improve your manuscript.

Take time to review feedback: Once you receive feedback, take the time to check it carefully. Consider each comment and decide which changes you want to make to your manuscript. Remember that not all input will be helpful or relevant, so you must use your judgment when determining which changes to make.

Getting a fresh perspective: After working on a manuscript for months or even years, seeing it with fresh eyes can be challenging. Having someone else read your work can give you a new perspective on your story and help you identify improvement areas.

Identifying problem areas: Friends and family can provide valuable feedback on areas of your manuscript that may not be clear or need more development. This can help you identify problems and make changes before publishing your book.

Building a fan base: Sending your book to friends and family can help you build a fan base before publication. If they enjoy your work, they may recommend it to others, allowing you to build momentum and generate interest in your book.

In summary, sending your finished book to friends and family for review can be a helpful step in the publishing process. By choosing your reviewers carefully, giving clear instructions, being open to criticism, and taking time to review feedback, you can use this process to identify problem areas, get a fresh perspective, and build a fan base.

Choose a review group from among family, friends, church members, peer groups, or others with experience in the writing field. Give each reviewer sufficient time to go through your book or specific chapters.

The Final Touch

Your book is now ready, checked by humans and technology, human intelligence, and artificial intelligence, and prepared to go into the oven of publication. The book has been carefully vetted and reviewed by people and technology, using a combination of human judgment and computer algorithms to identify errors, inconsistencies, and other issues.

If you have not yet created a paperback copy of your book, it is time to do it now. Make another copy of your original fully edited book and name it <Title of Book – paperback edition>. Rename the original book as <Title of Book – eBook edition>. Format each copy according to its type. The content in both documents should be the same, but they must be formatted according to the particular edition in which they will be published.

CHAPTER 5: DESIGNING YOUR BOOK COVER

THE FAMOUS SAYING IS, "Do not judge a book by its cover.". As a book writer, you will soon realise that the opposite is true.

You may have already written a great book as a first-time indie writer. However, having an eye-catching cover is as important as having great content. Your book cover is the first thing a potential reader sees, so it needs to be visually appealing and accurately represent the contents of your book. This chapter will discuss designing a book cover for eBook and paperback formats.

Understanding the Importance of a Good Book Cover.

A good book cover does more than attract a potential reader's attention as it conveys important information about the book, such as the genre, tone, and target audience. It also sets the reader's expectations about the book's content. For example, a book cover for a thriller novel may feature a dark, ominous design, while a romance novel may have a bright, romantic cover.

Choosing the Right Image.

The first step in designing a book cover is to choose the right image. This can be a photograph, a graphic design, or an illustration. It should be eye-catching and relevant to the content of your book.

If you're not an artist, you can hire a professional designer to create a custom image for your book cover. Several websites offer royalty-free stock images that you can use for your cover. However, remember that your chosen image should be unique and not too similar to other book covers in your genre. If you decide to use a photograph, make sure it is high-quality and has a high resolution. The image's resolution should be at least 300 dpi (dots per inch) to ensure it looks good on both eBook and paperback covers.

Choosing the Right Fonts.

The font you choose for your book cover should be easy to read and appropriate for the genre and tone of your book. For example, a thriller novel may have a bold, dramatic font, while a romance novel may have a flowing, elegant font. It's best to use a maximum of two fonts for your book cover to keep it visually appealing and easy to read. You can also use different font sizes and styles to emphasise certain words or phrases.

Designing the eBook cover

Remember that when designing your eBook cover, it will be displayed in a smaller size on online bookstores like Amazon. This means that the image and text on the cover should be clear and easy to read at a smaller size. The size of an eBook cover is typically 1600 x 2560 pixels. You can use graphic design software, such as Adobe Photoshop or Canva, to create your eBook cover. Alternatively, you can use online ebooks cover design tools like BookBrush or Cover Creator on Kindle Direct Publishing.

Ensure the title and author name are easy to read and stand out on the cover. You can also include a tagline or a brief book description to entice potential readers.

Designing the Paperback Cover.

When designing the paperback cover, you need to consider the spine and back cover in addition to the front cover. The spine will display the title, author name, and publisher logo, while the back cover can include a brief synopsis of the book, author bio, and reviews.

The size of a paperback cover depends on the dimensions of your book. You can use online book cover design templates like Canva or Blurb to create your paperback cover. Alternatively, you can hire a professional designer to create a custom cover.

Ensure that the text on the spine is readable when the book is on a bookshelf. The font size should be larger than the font size on the front cover. It's also essential to ensure that the back cover design complements the front cover design and that the information presented on the back cover is accurate and enticing.

Formatting Your Book Cover.

When formatting your book cover, you need to consider the platform's requirements where you will be publishing your book. For example, Amazon Kindle Direct Publishing has specific guidelines for cover dimensions and file types. It's vital to ensure that your cover meets these requirements to avoid any issues with the publishing process. You can find the guidelines for each platform on their website or by contacting their customer support.

Testing Your Book Cover.

Once you have designed your book cover, testing it to ensure it effectively attracts potential readers is crucial. You can do this by creating a mockup of your book cover and showing it to people in your target audience to get their feedback. You can also create a split test where you create two versions of your cover and see which one performs better in attracting potential readers.

Conclusion.

Designing a book cover is an essential aspect of indie publishing. A good book cover can attract potential readers and accurately represent the contents of your book. When designing your book cover, please choose the right image and fonts, consider the platform requirements, and test your design to ensure its effectiveness. By following these tips, you can create an eye-catching book cover that accurately represents your book and attracts potential readers more significantly than the font size used on the front cover.

Outsourcing Cover Design

Cover design is an art and an integral part of the success of your book. Outsourcing the cover design to a freelancer is recommended to ensure your book's best cover. Many websites provide a host of freelance cover designers who will do the work for a fee. One popular website is Fiverr.com. You can review the profiles of the listed designers and choose one with experience designing covers for books in your genre that meet your budget.

Most of these designers will produce the cover for eBooks, paperback, and Facebook and Instagram posts. The designer will be able to create an appropriate cover, provided you submit adequate details about your book, which would include the following –

The genre in which your book belongs and the kind of readers.

A brief write-up of the book's central theme is needed.

The title of the book and the name of the author/s should also be included.

A brief synopsis and author bio for the back cover of the paperback.

The most important information is the book page size you will select for publishing the paperback edition and the number of pages your book will contain. Once you have formatted the paperback document by choosing the page size layout, word will display the book's number of pages.

If you have any specific colour for the cover or image, please mention the same.

Outsourcing is the best option for first-time Indie authors as the complexity of the task can be avoided and left to a professional to handle.

CHAPTER 6: SELF-PUBLISHING

YOUR BOOK IS NOW FORMATTED, reviewed, and edited, ready to go Live.

Self-publishing has become increasingly popular as technology has made it easier for anyone to write, edit, and publish their book. Indie authors can take control of the entire publishing process, from writing to marketing, and earn more of their book's profits than traditional publishing.

In this chapter, we will explore the benefits of self-publishing by indie authors and why it might be the right choice for you.

Creative Control

One of the most significant advantages of self-publishing is the creative control it offers. As an indie author, you have complete control over the content of your book, from the writing to the cover design. You can make all the decisions about your book, including the title, cover, and marketing strategy. This creative control allows you to tell the story without interference from publishers or editors who may have a different vision for your book. You can take risks with your writing, experiment with different styles, and publish a book that is true to your vision.

Higher Royalties

Another significant advantage of self-publishing is that indie authors can earn more of their book's profits than traditional publishing. In traditional publishing, authors typically make a royalty rate of around 10-15% of the book's price. However, as a self-published author, you can earn up to 70% of your book's price, depending on your platform. This means you can make more money from your book, which can be especially beneficial for first-time authors who may not have a large audience yet.

Flexibility

Self-publishing also offers a lot of flexibility compared to traditional publishing. As an indie author, you can choose the format of your book, whether it's an ebook, paperback, or hardcover. You can also select the distribution channels and marketing strategy that works best for you. This flexibility allows you to adapt to changes in the market and reach your target audience more effectively. You can experiment with different pricing strategies, promotions, and marketing techniques until you find what works best for your book.

Speed to Market

Traditional publishing can take months or even years to get your book to market. As an indie author, you can publish your book much faster. You can write, edit, and publish your book within weeks or months, depending on how much time you dedicate. This speed to market can be especially beneficial for authors who want to take advantage of trends or current events. For example, if you write a book about a current topic or trend, you can get your book to market quickly and take advantage of the buzz.

Building a Brand

Self-publishing can also help you build your brand as an author. By publishing your book, you can establish yourself as an expert in your field and build a following of loyal readers. You can also use your book as a marketing tool to promote other products or services you offer. Building a brand as an author can take time and effort, but it can be a valuable asset in the long run. A strong brand can help you sell more books, attract more readers, and establish yourself as a thought leader in your field.

Community

Finally, self-publishing allows you to connect with other indie authors and build a community of like-minded individuals. There are many online communities and forums where indie authors can share their experiences, ask for advice, and support each other. This community can be a valuable resource for new authors who may feel overwhelmed by the publishing process. By connecting with other indie authors, you can learn from their experiences, get feedback on your writing, and build relationships to help you grow your audience.

KDP Amazon Publishing

This chapter will consider publishing using the Kindle Direct Publishing (KDP) platform.

First, you will have to create an account at KDP Amazon. If you already have an Amazon account, you can use the same credentials to log in to KDP, Amazon. Once logged in, you must create your account profile – Your legal name, Address, Date of Birth, Phone number, and business type (Individual or Corporation). The next step will be to add your Bank account details into which you will receive your royalty payments. Finally, you must complete Tax Information details depending on your country's tax laws. Upon completion of the profile, the system will generate an account ID. Please take note of it.

Before uploading your finished book on KDP, there are a few steps you need to complete beforehand. Prepare a short synopsis describing your book. Remember, the Amazon reader will read this on your book page to learn more about your book. It should capture the essence of your book's content and be catchy enough to hold the reader's attention and encourage a buying decision. Spend some time working on this brief; if needed, you can take the help of ChatGPT for this purpose.

Identify the categories in which you will upload your manuscript. Amazon allows the use of two categories when you first upload. Later you can add up to eight more categories. In addition to categories, Amazon allows the use of seven keywords. Categories and keywords are a subject on their own and are beyond this book's scope.

Once your manuscript is ready, log in to your KDP account, click the "Create a New Title" button, and select eBook. You will have to enter details under three tabs –

Kindle eBook Details

Kindle eBook Content

Kindle eBook Pricing

<u>Kindle eBook Details Tab:</u>

Select the language of your book from the drop-down list. Enter the book title and subtitle (optional). Ignore the series and edition number fields if this is your first book. Next, enter the name of the author and any contributors. The contributor field is optional, but if you have co-authors, photographers, editors, or others to credit for your book, you can select the contributor category and enter their names.

The following fields are important as they serve to market your book. Your book synopsis will go in the description box. This will appear on your book page for readers to learn more about your book and make a buying decision. Select "I own the copyright for the publishing rights" if you own the book. Enter up to seven keywords in the keyword field. This can be a single word or phrase. After that, choose two categories you want your book to be listed. After publication, you can add up to eight more categories. (Refer to Appendix – II, KDP Categories and keywords)

The age and grade range fields are optional. Select either pre-order or publish immediately, depending on your preference. For first-time writers, I recommend selecting "publish immediately". You can then click "Save as Draft" and exit to continue later or "Save and Continue" to proceed to the next tab.

Kindle eBook Content:

This is the tab where you will upload your manuscript and book cover. I strongly recommend first-time writers uncheck the Digital Rights Management (DRM) option in the manuscript section. Click the "Upload eBook manuscript" button and select your file, i.e., the <Title of Book – eBook Edition> eBook version. KDP will check for spelling errors and complete the processing of the file. If there are errors, you will need to correct them and re-upload the file.

In the next section, Kindle eBook cover, upload your book cover. The file should be either in jpg or tiff format. Once the uploads are complete without errors, you can launch the Previewer in the next section. The Previewer allows you to view the book as it appears on Kindle, mobile, and tablet devices in both vertical and horizontal modes. Verify all the pages; if satisfied, click "Approve".

For eBooks, ISBN is optional. Skip this section. You can then click "Save as Draft" and exit to continue later or "Save and Continue" to proceed to the next tab.

<u>Kindle eBook Pricing</u>:

If you enrol your book in the KDP Select program, you cannot publish the book on other self-publishing sites. Thankfully, the KDP Select enrollment is for a fixed duration of three months, after which you can continue to be enrolled for another three months or exit. If you enrol, your book will be available to KDP Unlimited members free of cost, and your royalty will be calculated based on the pages read. I recommend that first-time authors enrol in KDP Select.

Territories: Preferably choose All territories (worldwide) unless you have a reason for selecting specific territories. Select the primary marketplace where you would expect maximum sales.

The most important section is Pricing, Royalty, and Distribution. There are two royalty plans – 35% and 70%. To avail of 70%, you must price your book between USD 2.99 and 9.99. Any price below USD 2.99 will automatically be converted to a 35% royalty. KDP will alter the price to its respective currency in other marketplaces.

Finally, click "Publish Your Kindle eBook," KDP will review your book for publishing. It may take up to seventy-two hours, but generally, it will happen much earlier. I strongly recommend you click "Save as Draft" and allow a few days to review before committing to publication.

<u>Publishing paperback:</u>

Once your paperback manuscript is ready, log in to your KDP account. The Bookshelf section will display the eBook and paperback, with the eBook action "Setup complete" and the paperback action "Complete your setup". Click on "Complete Setup", and the three tabs similar to the eBook process will appear.

The first tab – Paperback Details – will be populated with the data entered for the eBook. The Print ISBN is the first section in the next tab – Paperback Content. Amazon provides writers with a free ISBN. If you don't have your own ISBN, click "Get a Free ISBN", and Amazon will immediately assign a new ISBN. Once you have an ISBN, you may mention it on the book's copyright page.

Leave the Publication date blank. The next section is the most important – Print Options. Select the trim size of your book based on the layout size of your Word document, and choose the other options as per your choice.

There is one significant difference between eBook and paperback upload of the manuscript. The Word document has to be converted into a PDF file, as this section will only accept a PDF manuscript. Next, upload your book cover. If there are any errors, you will have to correct them and re-upload them. Most mistakes relate to a book's trim size and cover design mismatch. Communicate the correct trim size and the number of book pages to the cover designer. Once the upload is successful, click "Launch Previewer" and verify your book page-by-page. At the bottom of the tab will appear your book's printing cost. This is important for determining the price in the next tab.

The last tab – Paperback Rights & Pricing – is where you set the price and view the royalty you will earn. Finally, you can request proof of your book, which will be available at cost. Once you receive your physical book, you can verify that it meets all your requirements before you commit the paperback to publish.

In conclusion, publishing a book on KDP Amazon is relatively simple. With careful planning and attention to detail, you can publish and promote your eBook and paperback to a global audience.

Congratulations, you are now an Indie Author. Welcome into the world of writers. Your journey has just begun.

THE ROAD TO SELF-PUBLISHING

CHAPTER 7: SUMMARY ROUNDUP

IF YOU HAVE A PASSION for writing, it's time to start the engine and take the necessary steps to get where you want to go. Here's a roadmap to help you on your journey:

<u>Planning</u>: Before starting your journey, you need to determine your destination and plan your route. Similarly, before beginning to write, you must decide what your book is about and plan your content. Research your target audience and the competition in your genre to help guide your writing. Planning and gathering your thoughts on the subject matter is a prolonged phase of your journey. Use Microsoft OneNote to gather the content for your book.

<u>Focus</u>: Once on the road, you must focus and stay alert. In writing, you must remain focused on your content and avoid getting sidetracked by writer's block or other distractions. Open a blank document in Word and start typing.

<u>Challenges</u>: As you drive, you will face bad weather, traffic jams, and detours. Similarly, you may encounter writer's block or struggle with language clarity and grammar errors in writing and self-publishing. But like a good driver, a successful writer can overcome challenges by staying focused and persistent. Tools like Grammarly and ChatGPT can assist in overcoming these challenges.

<u>Relax</u>: It's important to take breaks and rest during long drives. Writing for long periods without breaks can lead to burnout. Take breaks to recharge your creative energy and avoid becoming too fatigued to continue writing. Enjoy good music in between and go for a walk.

<u>Learning</u>: Driving, writing, and self-publishing require constant learning and improvement. Just as a driver needs to keep up with new road rules and driving techniques, a writer needs to keep up with recent trends and techniques in self-publishing. Attend workshops, read blogs, and network with other writers to improve your craft and stay ahead of the curve. Remember formatting rules, such as page breaks, layout size, margins, and automatic Table of contents.

<u>Honking</u>: Just like the car on the road announces its presence to other vehicles and pedestrians by honking, marketing strategies announce your book's presence to potential readers. This book does not cover the marketing subject as it is beyond the scope and requires a separate book for its treatment.

THE ROAD TO SELF-PUBLISHING

APPENDIX I: FOR INDIAN WRITERS

INDIAN WRITERS WHO want to reach out to Indian readers in paperback format may find they hit a roadblock. KDP does not make paperback editions available on Amazon.in. For Indian buyers to purchase from Amazon.com can be very costly as they will have to pay in dollars and have higher delivery costs.

Notion Press is an Indian website that provides Indian writers with a platform to convert their books into paperback format and make them available to Indian buyers through Amazon.in, Flipkart, and their website.

To start, open the webpage – notionpress.com and click "Get Started". Enter your name, email ID, Mobile Number and password. Your email ID and password become the login credentials. Click "Publish my book".

Select the language in which your book is written. Click "Finished writing, ready to Publish" and select "Publish on your own for Free". What follows is identical to the KDP process with minor changes. There are three tabs – Book Information, Book Content Design, Distribution & Pricing. After every tab page, click "Save Draft" or "Save and Continue."

Book Information:

Enter the title, subtitle, author name, contributors' names, and book genre here.

Book Content Design:

Here, decide on the book size, binding type, book interior, paper type, and cover lamination. Unlike KDP Amazon, you cannot upload your cover design directly. You will have to click "Launch cover creator". You can select how your front and back covers appear on the cover creator page. You can attach the file to the cover template if you already have a cover design. Text templates allow you to add the book's title and the author's name. But if your cover design has both title and author, remove the default text template from the front cover. You can use the back cover text template to add a short synopsis and author bio.

Next, upload your book manuscript in pdf format. Click "Save Draft" or "Save and Continue". The final step is the book's distribution and pricing. Set the price for the Domestic, i.e., Indian marketplace, based on the cost of production and the minimum price you can set. The author's earnings from Notion Press and other stores will be displayed based on your price. Enter a brief description of the book, author's biography, keywords, and categories in the following fields. This is your marketing tab, so carefully choose your words. Once satisfied, tick all the boxes under the terms and conditions and click "Submit for Review". You will hear from Notion Press after your book is approved and ready to go live.

Your book, once published, will also be listed on Amazon.in along with the eBook. Notion Press will also endeavour to list it on Flipkart and other websites.

69

APPENDIX II: KDP CATEGORIES AND KEYWORDS

KDP, OR KINDLE DIRECT Publishing, is Amazon's self-publishing platform that allows authors to publish their books in both eBook and paperback formats. Selecting the appropriate categories and keywords is one of the most important factors in making your book discoverable on Amazon. This article will discuss the categories and keywords used in KDP Amazon publishing for eBooks and paperbacks.

Amazon Categories

Amazon classifies books into many categories, subcategories, and sub-subcategories. Choosing the proper categories for your book is essential to reaching your target audience. The categories are in the KDP dashboard when creating your book listing.

When selecting categories for your book, it's essential to consider your book's genre and subject matter. Additionally, you should research the categories in which top-selling books in your genre are listed. This will give you a good idea of the most relevant categories to your book.

In KDP, you can select up to two categories for your eBook and post-publishing, you can add another eight categories. Remember that you should not use categories interchangeably with keywords, as they are different. Categories are broader classifications of your book, while keywords are specific terms that describe your book in more detail.

When publishing books on Amazon, keywords play an important role in getting discovered by potential readers. Keywords are the words or phrases that Amazon uses to index your book, making it easier for readers to find it when they search for a specific topic or genre.

Here are some tips for selecting the right keywords for your KDP Amazon book:

Brainstorm relevant keywords

Start by brainstorming a list of keywords that are relevant to your book. Think about the topics, themes, and genres that your book covers. For example, if you've written a novel mystery set in a small town, some relevant keywords might include "small town mystery," "whodunit," "detective," "crime fiction," and "suspense."

Use Amazon's autocomplete feature

Another way to develop relevant keywords is to use Amazon's autocomplete feature. When you start typing a keyword into the search bar on Amazon, the site will suggest a list of related keywords. For example, if you type in "small-town mystery," Amazon might suggest "small-town mysteries cosy," "small-town mysteries series," and "small-town mystery books."

Research your competition

Look at other books in your genre and see their keywords. You can do this by typing in relevant keywords and seeing which books appear in the search results. Please take note of their keywords and consider using some for your book.

Focus on long-tail keywords

Long-tail keywords are longer, more specific, and less competitive phrases than shorter, broader ones. For example, "small-town mystery" is a broad keyword, while "small-town mystery set in the 1950s" is a more specific long-tail keyword. While long-tail keywords may have a lower search volume, they can be more effective in discovering your book by readers looking for a particular topic or genre.

Don't use irrelevant keywords

It's important to use keywords that are relevant to your book. Don't try to game the system by using keywords unrelated to your book to get more visibility. Doing so violates Amazon's terms of service and may result in removing your book from the site.

Use all seven keyword slots

Amazon allows you to enter up to seven keywords for your book. Use all seven slots to maximize your book's visibility. Make sure each keyword is unique and relevant to your book.

Test and refine your keywords

Keywords aren't set in stone. If you do not see the desired results, try changing your keywords and seeing if that makes a difference. You can also use Amazon's advertising platform to test keywords and see which performs best.

In summary, selecting the right keywords for your KDP Amazon book is crucial for getting discovered by potential readers.

Publisher Rocket (KDP Rocket):

Publisher Rocket is a software tool available at publisherrocket.com that allows you to review different KDP categories and their impact on book sales. It displays the number of books that must be sold to reach the Number 1 and Number 10 ranks in a specific category. Choosing a category with lower total sales can increase your chances of achieving a rank between one and ten.

The tool also provides keyword and competition analysis in your book genre. However, it's not available for free and requires a one-time payment. But it can help rocket your book's discoverability and sales to a new level.

pg.

75

Don't miss out!

Visit the website below and you can sign up to receive emails whenever MATHEW THOMAS publishes a new book. There's no charge and no obligation.

https://books2read.com/r/B-A-TUWX-WTVHC

BOOKS 2 READ

Connecting independent readers to independent writers.

www.ingramcontent.com/pod-product-compliance
Lightning Source LLC
Chambersburg PA
CBHW071500130726
47997CB00006B/2414